A GIFT FOR

Nelly & Ken

FROM

Dad & Rothann

Awaiting the big day!

The Baby Blessing

HELEN EXLEY GIFTBOOKS:
for the most thoughtful gifts of all

OTHER GIFTBOOKS BY HELEN EXLEY

My Daughter, my joy...
A Special Collection in Praise of Mothers
To my Daughter with Love
Welcome to the New Baby
Thoughts on... Being a Mother
To a very special Daughter
To a very special Dad
Thoughts on... Being a Father
To my Grandmother with Love
To a very special Grandmother
To a very special Grandpa
Sons...
A Christening Gift
Baby Record Book
Welcome to Your New Baby Girl
Welcome to Your New Baby Boy

Published simultaneously in 2001 by Exley Publications Ltd
in Great Britain, and Exley Publications LLC in the USA.

2 4 6 8 10 12 11 9 7 5 3

Selection and arrangement copyright © Helen Exley 2001.
The moral right of the author has been asserted.

ISBN 1-86187-205-4

Words and pictures selected by Helen Exley.
Pictures researched by Image Select International.
Printed in China.

To the babies in my life.
They are little Kezia and Jasper.
H E L E N

Exley Publications Ltd, 16 Chalk Hill, Watford, Herts WD1 4BN, UK.
Exley Publications LLC, 232 Madison Avenue, Suite 1409, NY 10016, USA.

THE BABY BLESSING

A HELEN EXLEY GIFTBOOK

NEW YORK • WATFORD, UK

A NEW BABY
IS LIKE THE BEGINNING
OF ALL THINGS —
WONDER, HOPE,
A DREAM OF POSSIBILITIES.

EDA LESHAN

... the beginning of all things

Something to live for came to place
Something to die for maybe

Something to give even sorrow a grace
And yet it was only a baby

HARRIET SPOFFORD

*Every child comes with the message
that God is not yet discouraged.*

RABINDRANATH TAGORE (1861-1941)

Before you were conceived
I wanted you
Before you were born
I loved you
Before you were here an hour
I would die for you
This is the miracle of life.

MAUREEN HAWKINS

a new-born child

Of all the joys that lighten
suffering earth,
what joy is welcomed like a new-born child?

CAROLINE NORTON (1808-1877)

DAWN IS THE CHILD
WET WITH BIRTH.

CHARLOTTE DE CLUE, FROM "MORNING SONG"

*Life is a flame
that is always burning itself out,
but it catches fire again
every time a baby is born.*

GEORGE BERNARD SHAW (1856-1950)

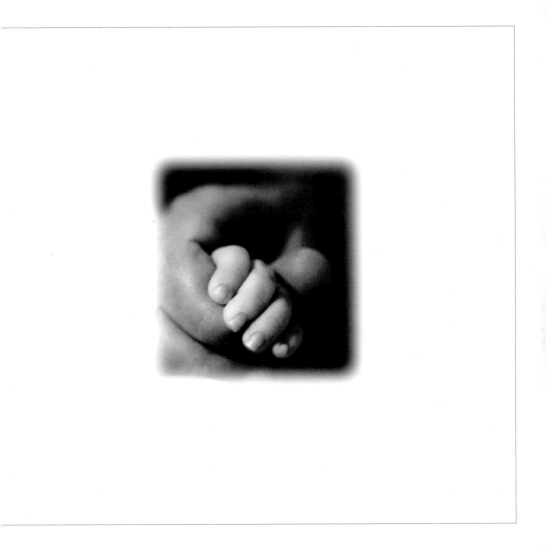

...to hold our hearts...

forever

Small child – once you were a hope, a dream.

Now you are reality.

Changing all that is to come.

So small. A flick of star stuff.

A mind to touch the edges of the universe.

A love to hold our hearts forever.

CHARLOTTE GRAY, B.1937

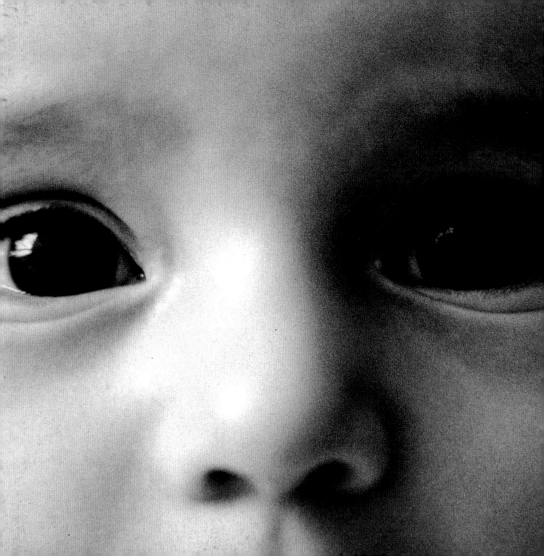

... and I held her for the first time

the first time

*T*hen they handed her to me, stiff and
howling, and I held her for the first time
and kissed her, and she went still and quiet as
though by instinctive guile, and I was instantly
enslaved by her flattery of my powers.

LAURIE LEE (1914-1997), FROM "TWO WOMEN"

She was born, squawling and berating the air,

her face stripped of its wisdom and serenity.

... Then someone placed her in my arms.

She looked up at me. Recognition, a memory

of two souls. She relaxed. The crying stopped.

Her eyes melted through me, forging a connection

in me with their soft heat. I felt her love power

stir in my heart.

SHIRLEY MACLAINE, B.1934,
FROM "DANCE WHILE YOU CAN"

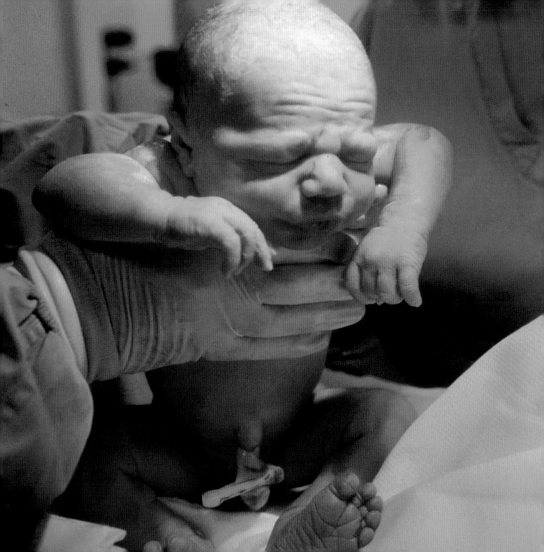

Newborn, of course, she looked already a centenarian,
tottering on the brink of an old crone's grave,
exhausted, shrunken, bald as Voltaire, mopping, mowing,
and twisting wrinkled claws in speechless spasms
of querulous doom.

LAURIE LEE (1914-1997), FROM "TWO WOMEN"

I'LL NEVER FORGET THE FIRST TIME
I SAW YOU. YOU WERE WET, STICKY,
WRINKLY AND SCREAMING YOUR
HEAD OFF. THE MOST PERFECT,
BEAUTIFUL SIGHT I HAD EVER SEEN.

STUART MACFARLANE

I'll carry your first cry
with me everywhere I go.

PAULA D'ARCY

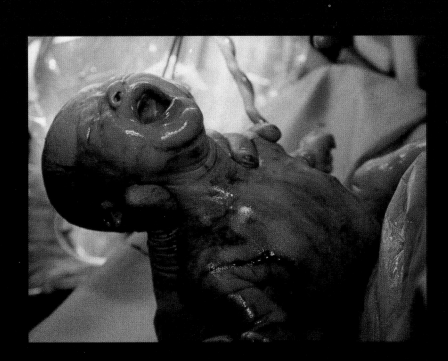

... what life means

NO MAN CAN POSSIBLY KNOW WHAT LIFE MEANS,

WHAT THE WORLD MEANS, WHAT ANYTHING

MEANS, UNTIL HE HAS A CHILD AND LOVES IT.

AND THEN THE WHOLE UNIVERSE CHANGES

AND NOTHING WILL EVER AGAIN SEEM EXACTLY

AS IT SEEMED BEFORE.

LAFCADIO HEARN (1850-1904)

EVERY BABY BORN INTO THE WORLD IS

A FINER ONE THAN THE LAST.

CHARLES DICKENS (1812-1870)

SHE IS YOURS TO HOLD IN YOUR
CUPPED HANDS, TO GUARD AND TO
GUIDE. GIVE HER YOUR STRENGTH
AND WISDOM AND ALL THE GOOD
THAT LIFE CAN OFFER. YOURS IS A
SACRED TRUST. NEVER HARM HER WITH
WORDS THAT CAN BITE AND STING.
LEAD HER INTO TRUTH.

MICHELE GUINNESS, FROM "TAPESTRY OF VOICES"

a sacred trust

A BABY IS GOD'S OPINION THAT LIFE SHOULD GO ON.

CARL SANDBURG (1878-1967)

How small. How beautiful.
Whatever happens
in the years to come.
This is perfection.
This is love.

PAM BROWN, B.1928

IN ADORATION OF ALL BABIES

*A baby overwhelms us with its lovableness;
even its smell stirs us more deeply than the smell
of pine or baking bread. What is overpowering
is simply the fact that a baby is life.*

BILL COSBY, B.1937, FROM "FATHERHOOD"

*"Henry Rackmeyer, you tell us what is important."
"A shaft of sunlight at the end of a dark afternoon,
a note in music, and the way the back
of a baby's neck smells...."*

E.B. WHITE (1899-1985)

A SWEET CHILD
IS THE SWEETEST THING
IN NATURE.

CHARLES LAMB (1775-1834)

BORN IN LOVE.
BORN TO LOVE.

STUART AND LINDA MACFARLANE

you love him even more

... one thing about having a baby,
is that each step of the way, you simply
cannot imagine loving him any more
than you already do,
because you are bursting with love,
loving as much
as you are humanly capable of,
and then you do; you love him
even more.

ANNE LAMOTT

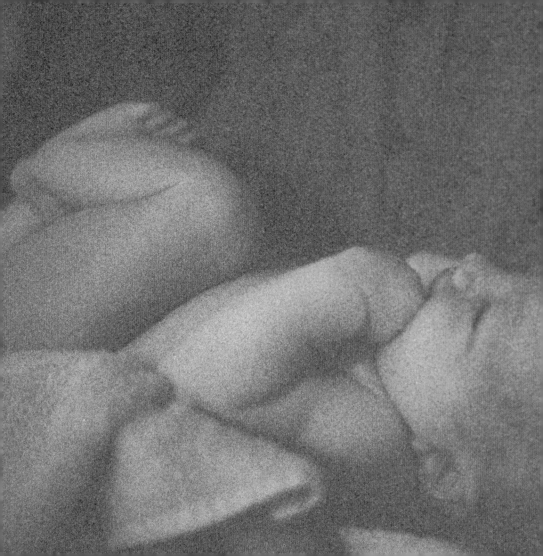

*There is nothing on earth like
the moment of seeing one's first baby.
Men scale other heights,
but there is no height like
this simple one,
occurring continuously throughout
all the ages in musty bedrooms,
in palaces, in caves and desert places.
I looked at this rolled-up bundle...
and knew again I had not
created her. She was herself
apart from me.
She had her own life to lead,
her own destiny to accomplish;
she just came past me
to this earth.*

KATHERINE TREVELYAN,
FROM "THROUGH MINE OWN EYES"

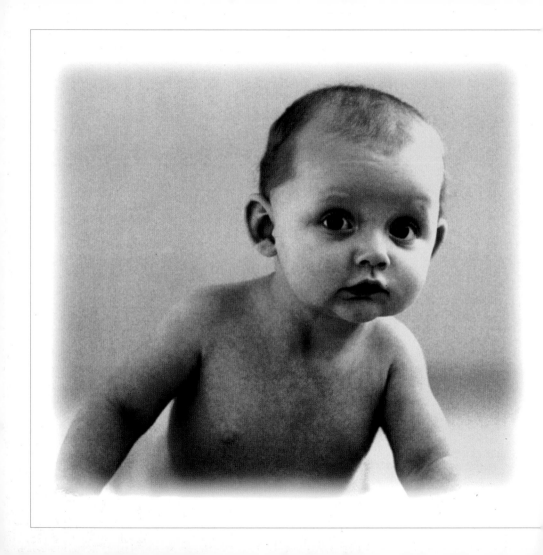

[My DAUGHTER]

from the moment she was born,

drew from me reserves of tenderness,

protectiveness and fight I never knew

I possessed. I wanted to change the world

overnight to make it a safer, easier

better place....

MICHELE GUINNESS, FROM "TAPESTRY OF VOICES"

so young

IN EVERY WORK THE BEGINNING

IS THE MOST IMPORTANT PART,

ESPECIALLY IN DEALING WITH ANYTHING YOUNG

AND TENDER.

SOCRATES (469-399 B.C.)

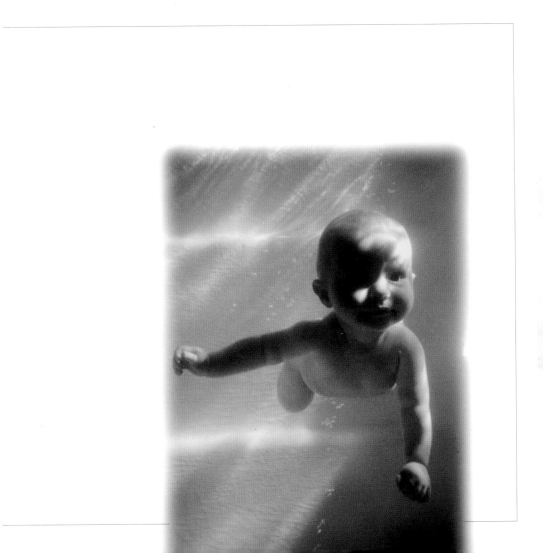

Having a child together — building a family together —
seemed a natural progression to the union
we began on our wedding day.
This little person is, among many other things,
a representation of our love for and commitment
to one another.

TRISH PERRY

two people in love

Yes, having a child
is surely the most beautifully
irrational act that two people
in love can commit.

BILL COSBY, B.1937

WHEN WE HEAR THE BABY LAUGH,
IT IS THE LOVELIEST THING
THAT CAN HAPPEN TO US.

SIGMUND FREUD (1856-1939)

When we hear the baby laugh

... in that moment of desperation
she let fly her first real smile: not a shy, average,
half-moon smile — but an open-mouthed,
toothless, silly wide gas of delight. She chortled at me,
and despite my stupor, I laughed back.
She'd taken me by surprise, and exhaustion dropped away,
flooded out on waves of pure maternal bliss.
... the spirit — that wild sense of humour — had been Anna
and stayed Anna from that minute on.

LINDA GRAY SEXTON

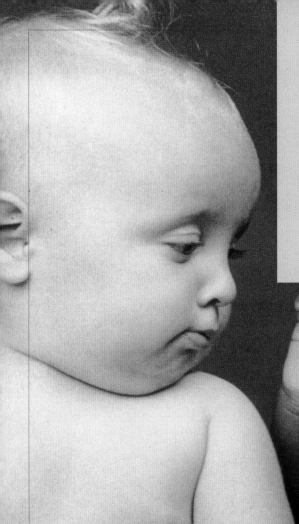

BABIES
ARE SUCH
A NICE WAY
TO START
PEOPLE.

DON HEROLD

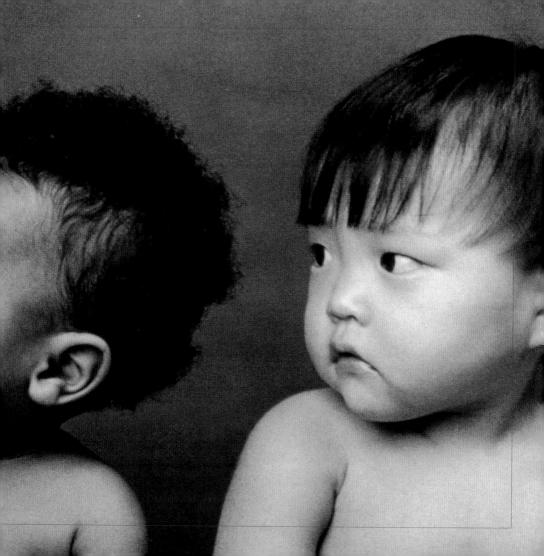

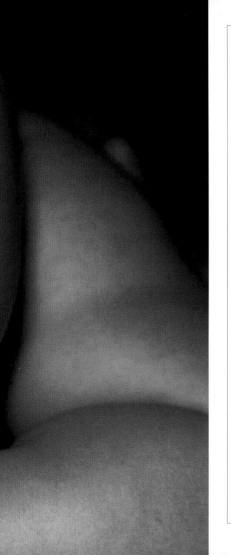

AT THREE IN THE MORNING
A BABY HITS ITS HIGH IN SMILES
AND CONVERSATION.

MAYA V. PATEL, B.1943

*I've patiently tried to explain
the schedule around here,
but a lopsided smile from this little
wizard and I find
the schedule won't work
any more. I've tried to go about
business as usual,
but it's hard with warm,
fat fingers tying up both
my hands.*

JUNE MASTERS BACHER,
FROM "THE GRANDMOTHER BOOK"

A baby up to no good can,
without a word,
exclaim: "Me? But I'm only a baby!"

PAM BROWN, B.1928

Long before speech,
a baby has learned that Charm Pays.

CHARLOTTE GRAY, B.1937

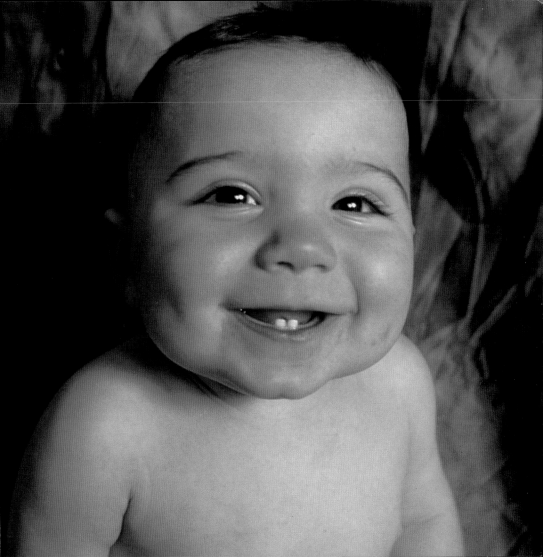

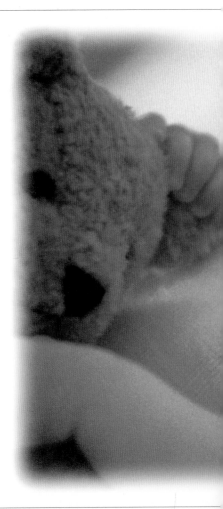

Dad has long and earnest conversations with his baby daughter. He tells her she is noisy, undisciplined and manipulative and she will be sent back if she doesn't pull herself together. And the baby smiles complacently. She has him exactly where she wants him.

PAM BROWN, B.1928

a baby's power

... when she cried her deep soulful cry,
I was filled not merely with panic
but with passion.

SUE LIMB, FROM "LOVE FORTY"

If children knew, oh, if they only knew
their power! It is something
absolutely glorious in its immensity.

ALINE KILMER (1888-1941)

so small, so soft...

SUCH TINY HANDS
TO HOLD OUR HEARTS FOREVER.

PAM BROWN, B.1928

What feeling is so nice
as a child's hand in yours?
So small, so soft and warm,
like a kitten huddling in the shelter
of your clasp.

MARJORIE HOLMES

How can one say no to a child?
How can one be anything
but a slave to one's own flesh and blood?

HENRY MILLER (1891-1980)

To care for a child was not an alien duty
imposed on me by a hostile culture,
it was rather the core,
the emotional wellspring,
the gravity that held my soul in place.

ANNE ROIPHE, FROM "A MOTHER'S EYE"

again and

When I hold her exhausted from the day's work

and the disturbed nights, there is a deep relief

and pleasure at finding myself able to give — again

and again — what's needed: bottles, changes, attention.

I've at last found the good mother within me,

the ability to put someone else's needs before my own,

and she's so beautiful it feels like a privilege.

again and again

JEAN RADFORD, FROM "BALANCING ACTS"

A CHILD'S LOVE AND TRUST

IT IS THE MOST OVERWHELMING EXPERIENCE
IN A PARENT'S LIFE – TO FEEL
THE ABSOLUTE TRUST, THE CERTAINTY
OF COMFORT, YOUR LITTLE CHILD'S
BELIEF IN YOUR OMNIPOTENCE.

PETER GRAY, B.1928

*Gradually I began to realise that she liked me, that she had
no option to liking me, and that unless I took great pains
to alienate her she would go on liking me....*
*It was very pleasant to receive such uncritical love,
because it left me free to bestow love; my kisses were met
by small warm rubbery unrejecting cheeks and soft dovey
mumblings of delight.*

MARGARET DRABBLE, B.1939, FROM "THE MILLSTONE"

During the first six months, the baby has

the rudiment of a love language available to him.

There is the language of the embrace,

the language of the eyes, the language of the smile,

vocal communications of pleasure and distress.

It is the essential vocabulary of love

before we can speak of love.

SELMA FRAIBERG

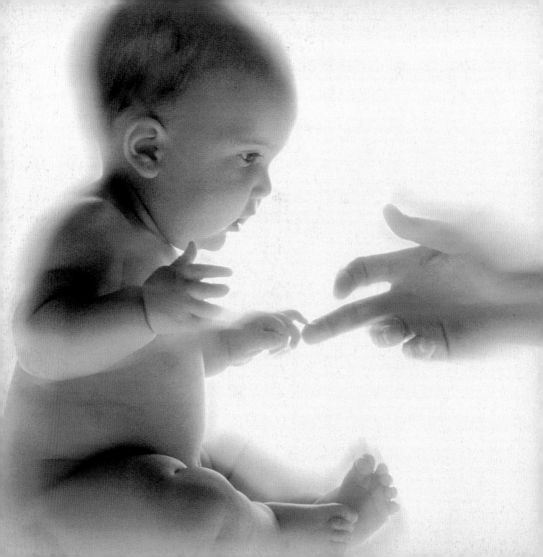

DEAR BABY

Every child is more precious and more
wonderful than all the wonders of the universe –
more intricate than every swirl of suns –
more capable of change and growth
and new creation.
And for we who love you – of all those children,
you are the most valued, the most
necessary to our joy.
Your eyes will see, your mind explore,
your heart will love, your hands create.
Be glad of life – of this extraordinary gift.

PAM BROWN, B.1928

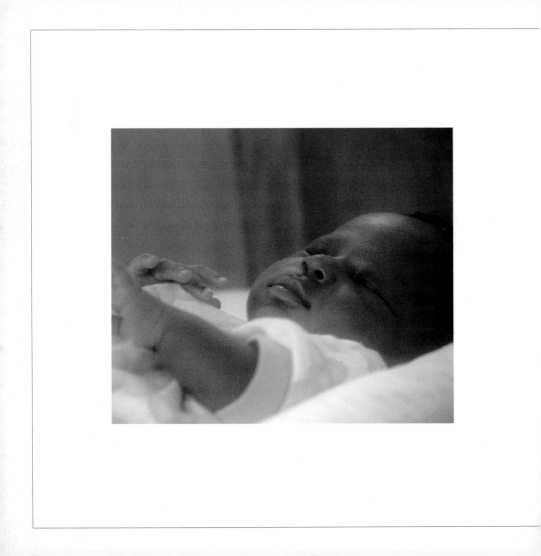

mending my heart

... I also had no idea
I could feel so deeply,
or that tucking children in
would have the serenity of prayer,
or that being their father
would renovate my heart.

HUGH O'NEILL,
FROM "A MAN CALLED DADDY"

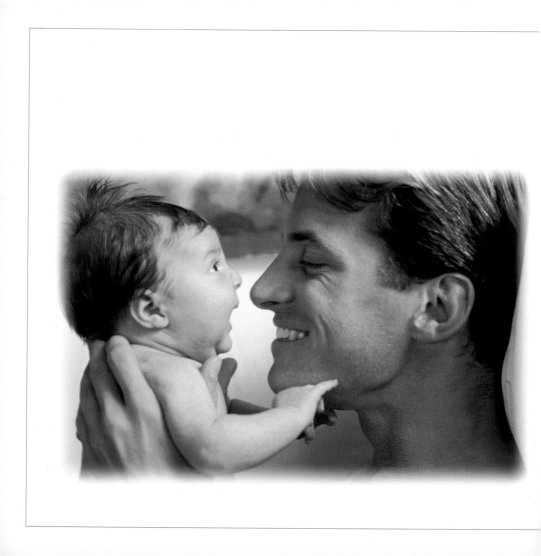

He is totally transformed by his first daughter. There is a gentleness about him that even love never discovered. He holds her like a flower, like thinnest glass. He wonders at this new and lovely life, incredible in its perfection.

PAM BROWN, B.1928

I used to love watching them together. He didn't know quite what to do with her – he would gaze at her with wonder in his eyes. She was delicate, she was a girl, so he would be delicate with her. He was a gentle man, not overly demonstrative, yet when he looked at his daughter you could see him melt. He became totally vulnerable.

LAUREN BACALL, B.1924, FROM "NOW"

another chance at life

*Y*ou were my life. When you arrived – small, defenceless,
with no one in the world but me – you invaded this silent,
sad house with your sudden bursts of laughter, your tears.
I can remember watching your big baby head oscillating
between the sofa and the table, and thinking that not
everything had ended. Chance, with its unforeseeable
generosity, had given me another bite at the cherry.

SUSANNA TAMARO

Just for a little while a human being
loves and trusts the world,
is amazed by its simplicities,
in awe of its complexities,
enchanted by light and colour, movement,
strangeness, eager to explore,
in love with waking and with sleeping.
Those who snatch away even one moment
of that golden time
have stolen something
that can never be replaced.

PAM BROWN, B.1928

that golden time

How a baby enjoys discovery.
It wriggles and squirms with joy,
reaches out its arms to hug the magic close
– the wind in the leaves, a shaft of sunlight,
a bird, a fish, a coloured puddle.
It lives in a world of amazement.

PAM BROWN, B.1928

Don't forget that compared
to a grown-up person every baby is a genius.
Think of the capacity to learn!
The freshness, the temperament,
the will of a baby a few months old!

MAY SARTON (1912-1995)

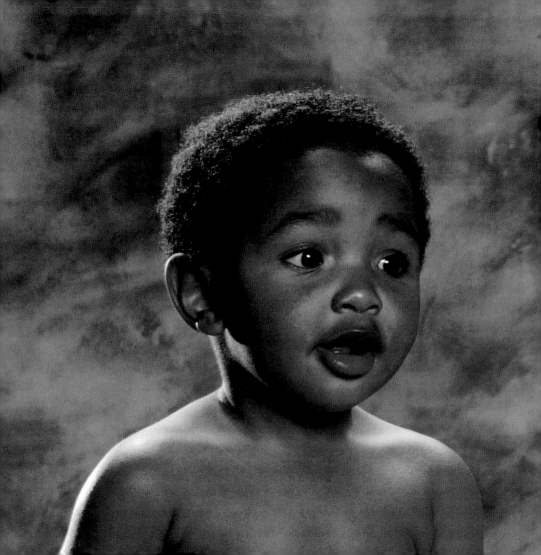

Her face lights up
when you — most ordinary you — come into sight.
Your songs delight her.
You are the one who can soothe her into sleep,
drive off her terrors, lever her from tears
to laughter. She is so beautiful, so funny,
so eager, so resolute.
And she loves you with all her heart.

PAM BROWN, B.1928

she loves you with all her heart

The baby has learned to smile, and her smiles
burst forth like holiday sparklers, lighting our hearts.
Joy fills the room.
At what are we smiling?
We don't know, and we don't care.
We are communicating with one another in happiness,
and the smiles are the outward display
of our delight and our love.

JOAN LOWERY NIXON,
FROM "THE GRANDMOTHER'S BOOK"

A baby is a great ego booster to grandparents when needed most – to a grandchild one is considered beautiful, brainy and is implored to sing another song, no matter how poor a singer – and one is made to feel the greatest story-teller of all times.

DORIS M. BRIDGE

new life!

THOU, STRAGGLER INTO LOVING ARMS,
YOUNG CLIMBER UP OF KNEES,
WHEN I FORGET THY THOUSAND WAYS,
THEN LIFE AND ALL SHALL CEASE.

MARY LAMB (1764-1847)

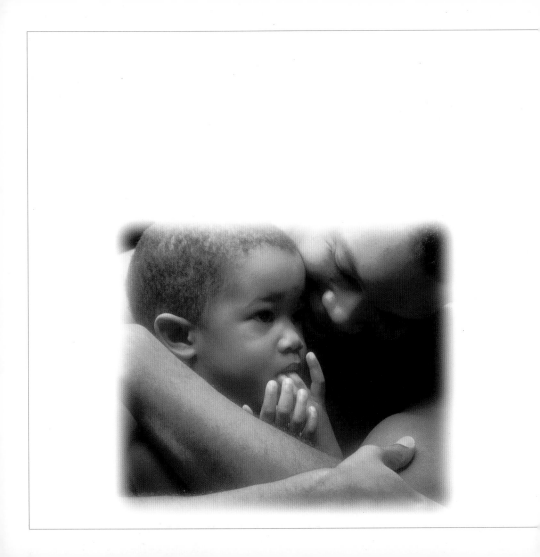

He feels with her – each restlessness, each fear, each pain. She laughs and he is overjoyed. She reaches out her little arms to him and he rejoices. She sleeps on his shoulder and he does not move, for fear of waking her. He shows her marvels and lives her astonishment in bird and cat and falling leaf. He asks for kisses. Hugs. The invisible gifts that she bestows on those she loves – held carefully between minute thumb and finger.

PAM BROWN, B.1928

a father is born

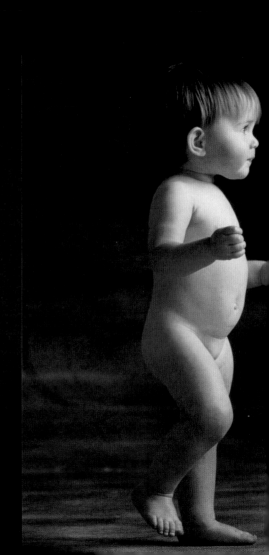

Here she comes, luminous
with pride, on her feet
and moving. She stops,
lurches, collapses neatly.
Beams. Reorganizes.
Up again. Come on, now
you can do it!
And she does – standing,
rocking slightly, clutching
at your knees.
I really think that that
deserves a jelly baby.
And a kiss.

PAM BROWN, B.1928

Small child. Clear crystal. Bright and clear.

Faceted as none before you.

Catching the light from every lovely thing

and turning it to rainbow.

Reflecting beauty back into the world.

Making all things new.

PAM BROWN, B.1928

all things new

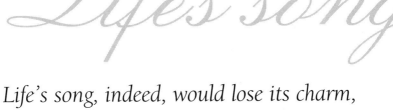

Life's song, indeed, would lose its charm,
Were there no babies to begin it;
A doleful place this world would be,
Were there no little people in it.

J.G. WHITTIER (1807-1892)

WHERE CHILDREN ARE,
THERE IS THE GOLDEN AGE.

NOVALIS (1772-1801)

She looks around her

and as she looks

She renews all she sees.

The leaves rustle excitedly,

The curtains dance by the window,

The shadow moves beside her as

She turns and she turns

and she turns,

Ocean eyes,

Taking it all in.

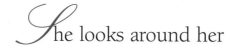

SALLY EMERSON, FROM "BACK TO WORK"

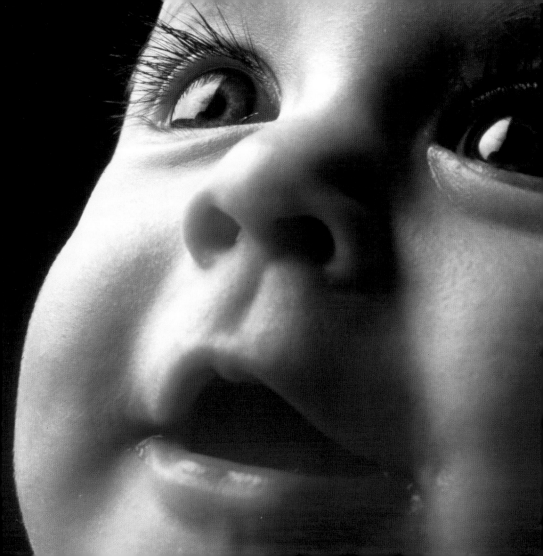

THAT FIRST SMILE

It was an extraordinary moment: something electric.
It was as if somebody had just come into the room.
Up till now, we'd admired her quiet alertness
and her wakeful curiosity, but had received from her
nothing but a rather stern stare. It was as if, all at once,
she was a person at last: had joined us.
This smile wreathed itself about my heart.
It was the moment of a lifetime, never to be forgotten.
I felt ravished by some divine spark of joy.

SUE LIMB, FROM "LOVE FORTY"

moment of a lifetime

BABIES STICK TO THE RULES. THEIR OWN.

PAM BROWN, B.1928

Melinda is a knockout.
... Yesterday she threw quite a tantrum
while out shopping
because I wouldn't let her handle the wheel of the car.
I tried to explain to her in small words
that the police disapprove of babies
fifteen months old driving Cadillacs,
but she was furious....

GROUCHO MARX (1895-1977), FROM "LOVE, GROUCHO"

YAA-AA-AAAA

*It demonstrates the power
of one very small child
when yours throws a tremendous tantrum
in the middle of the supermarket.*

PAM BROWN, B.1928

*If a baby is going to disgrace you
it will only be on an occasion
of extreme importance.*

PETER GRAY

KETCHUP!

A tiny daughter seems like a dolly to dress
but dolls do not sick, poo, dribble or
apply liberal quantities of paint and mud.
Satins and laces don't last long on this living doll.

PAMELA DUGDALE

SPAGHETTI!

My son favored the Dwight Eisenhower style
so popular with babies,
consisting of approximately eight wisps of hair
occasionally festooned with creamed spinach.

DAVE BARRY

CREAMED SPINACH!

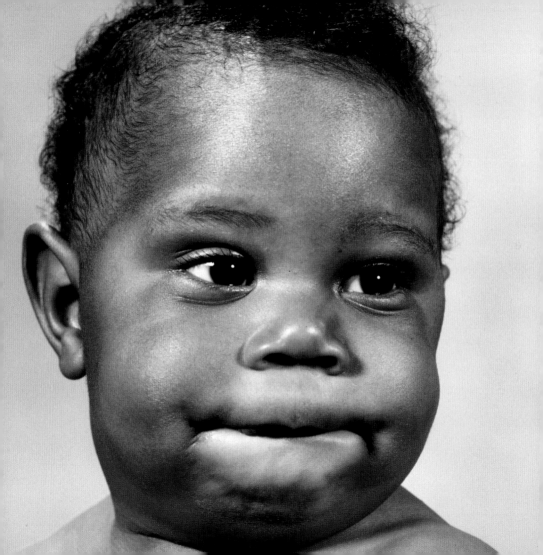

Being a parent is like being the agent of a self-centred Hollywood star. Your client says he doesn't like the script because it doesn't make him look sexy enough, or clever enough. You quietly work at convincing him to do the role. You feed his ego. Self-respect, pride and dignity are as important at three as they are at thirty-three. Like any business deal, the best way of winning is showing your opponent a dignified way of giving you exactly what you want. "I want you to have your bath and go to bed. You need guidance to understand that really that's what you want also."

NIGEL PLANER, FROM "A GOOD ENOUGH DAD"

Odd little people! They are the unconscious comedians of the world's great stage. They supply the humour in life's all too heavy drama. Each one, a small but determined opposition to the order of things in general, is for ever doing the wrong thing, at the wrong time, in the wrong place, and in the wrong way. ... Give an average baby a fair chance, and if it doesn't do something it oughtn't to, a doctor should be called in at once.

JEROME K. JEROME (1859-1927),
FROM "THE IDLE THOUGHTS OF
AN IDLE FELLOW"

chuckles!

*With a cheeky gurgle and a playful chuckle
you captured everyone's heart.*

STUART AND LINDA MACFARLANE

guffaws!

*Babies have laughs that are totally inappropriate
to their size —
huge guffaws, rumbles of delight,
squeals of excitement, rich and rounded gigglings.*

PAM BROWN, B.1928

giggles!

... I had discovered true love. The love which repays slavery
and exhaustion with a brief smile. But what a smile!
It was more than enough. My present prostration was
somehow sweeter than all the pleasures of my past life.

SUE LIMB, FROM "LOVE FORTY"

I cannot tell you exactly when I truly felt love for her.
I suspect it developed slowly over the first few weeks.
I know that by the time she started smiling at me
I felt not only love, but adulation.

CAROLYN JACOBS, ADOPTIVE MOTHER

When a baby first...

laughs that deep, unselfconscious gurgle;

or when it cries and you pick it up

and it clings sobbing to you, saved from some terrible

shadow moving across the room, or a loud clang

in the street, or perhaps, already, a bad dream:

then you are – happy is not the precise word – filled...

at the blind true core of life.

MARILYN FRENCH, B.1929, FROM "THE WOMEN'S ROOM"

THE LOVE OF A LITTLE CHILD

I LOVE THESE LITTLE PEOPLE;
AND IT IS NOT A SLIGHT THING
WHEN THEY, WHO ARE SO FRESH
FROM GOD, LOVE US.

CHARLES DICKENS (1812-1870)

*No one on earth
really deserves a baby's radiant smile
of recognition.*

CHARLOTTE GRAY, B.1937

Enchanting is that baby-laugh,

all dimples and glitter — so strangely warm and innocent.

MARGARET F. OSSOLI (1810-1850)

formed for joy

LITTLE CREATURE,
FORMED FOR JOY AND MIRTH.

WILLIAM BLAKE (1757-1827)

Her laugh is as wide and wise as winter.

There is nothing filmy nor flimsy about her.

JENNIFER MAIDEN, FROM "THE WINTER BABY"

with all of humanity

*There is nothing like raising a baby to make a person feel,
every day, like part of a mutual endeavor shared with all
of humanity and to realize the miraculous effort of love
that goes into the perpetuation of the human race.*

CAROL, A MOTHER OF GROWN CHILDREN
WHEN SHE ADOPTED A BABY,
FROM "LETTERS TO OUR DAUGHTERS"

I am hers to be with

*Having a child alters the rights of every man,
and I don't expect to live as I did without her.
I am hers to be with, and hope to be what she needs,
and know of no reason why I should ever desert her.*

LAURIE LEE (1914-1997), FROM "I CAN'T STAY LONG"

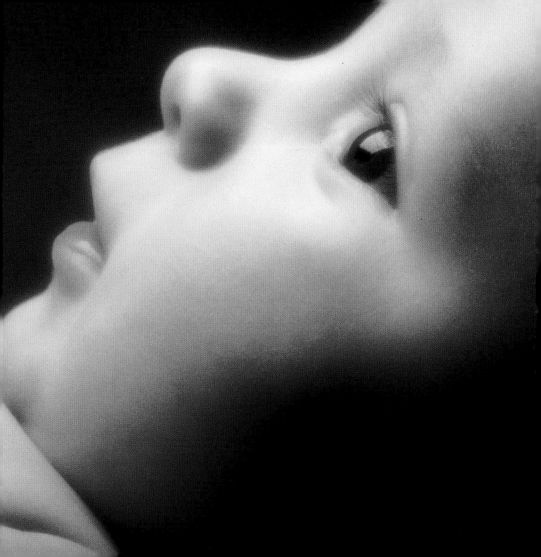

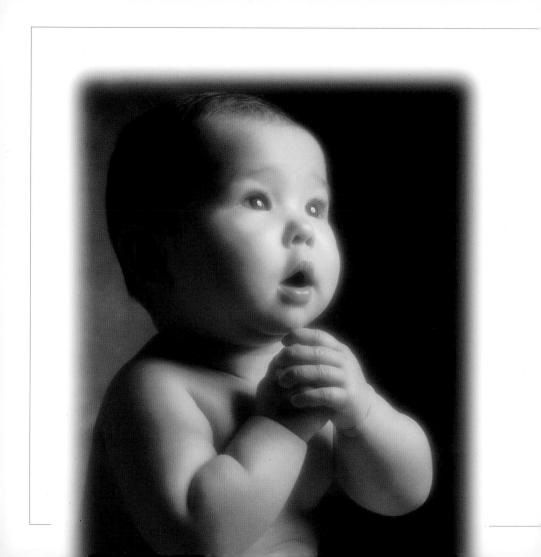

Dear child. I will care for you,
protect you – until you are grown.
And then I will let you fly free.
But, loving you? That is for always.

CHARLOTTE GRAY, B.1937

I will protect you

No ONE TELLS YOU
THAT THE CHANGE
IS IRREVERSIBLE.
THAT YOU WILL FEEL
IN YOUR HEART
EVERY PAIN, EVERY LOSS,
EVERY DISAPPOINTMENT,
EVERY REBUFF,
EVERY CRUELTY
THAT SHE EXPERIENCES
LIFE LONG.

PAM BROWN, B.1928

whenever you need my love

MY LOVE WILL BE WITH YOU
WHENEVER YOU NEED IT — FEEL ITS CARESS.

MY LOVE WILL BE WITH YOU
WHEN LIFE'S JOYS FILL YOUR HEART TO EXPLODING POINT.

MY LOVE WILL BE WITH YOU
WHEN LIFE'S WOES WEIGH YOU DOWN.

MY LOVE WILL BE WITH YOU
WHEN LIFE IS FEARFUL.

MY LOVE WILL BE WITH YOU
TODAY AND FOREVER.

STUART MACFARLANE

LIFE BEGINS AGAIN

... a baby brings out the love,
tolerance and tenderness
which has become rusty with the years.

F.M. WIGHTMAN

... when you see a new birth,
not just for yourself,
but for your children,
and then for their children –
somehow you stop questioning
and just know there's
a purpose to all our lives.

ROSEMARY WELLS,
FROM "YOUR GRANDCHILD AND YOU"

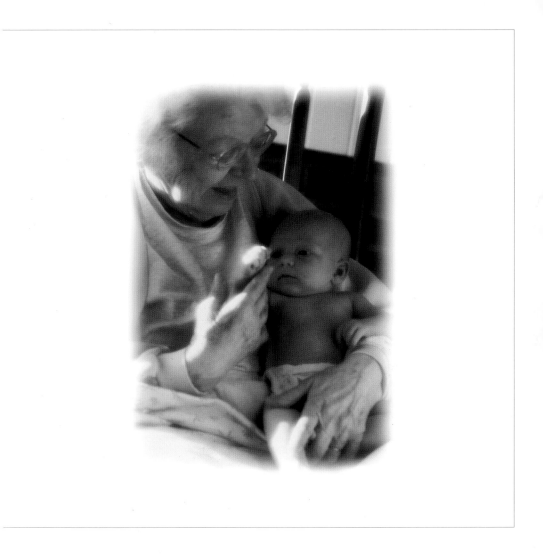

Hush Baby!

I will keep you safe.

Though the winds of the world

buffet at the door.

I will keep you safe till you are grown

and strong enough to stand alone.

And even then I will always be here

as comfort, refuge, breathing space,

when you need me as long as you need me.

With love, a listening ear....

Always.

I will keep you safe

PAM BROWN, B.1928

... the joyous gift

How I have prayed that no biting, stinging word

of mine, no inadvertent word of bitterness or sarcasm,

jealousy or malice, would poison or diminish the joyous,

loving, laughing gift I have held....

MICHELE GUINNESS, FROM "TAPESTRY OF VOICES"

You will never be free again. You live two lives now, hers and your own. And the greatest pain is having to let her make her own choices – whatever your experience foretells. Mercifully, this life link carries happiness as well as heartache. You are allowed to touch her joys, to share the triumphs and excitements. Distance cannot divide you. There will be nights without sleep. Days of waiting for a word. But letters. Unexpected phone calls. The astonishment of her standing on the doorstep when you thought her half a world away. And happiness beyond anything you ever thought possible. Surprises. Amazement. For she is your diamond daughter. She can cut across your heart and mind.

ROSANNE AMBROSE-BROWN, B.1943

You are all new.
As yet you are content
with such a little world –
discovering the air, the light,
the blur of faces.
But every day expands
your universe – and I will share
your joy. I have a new vocation –
to introduce you to this planet!

PAM BROWN, B.1928

My wish for you, little one

I wish you so much.
But most of all I wish you to be your own true self.
To take all the gifts that you were born with
and make of them marvels of beauty
and ingenuity and astonishment.

PAM BROWN, B.1928

A baby costs more
than anything else on earth.
Your love, your life.

HELEN THOMSON, B.1943

ACKNOWLEDGEMENTS

Exley Publications are grateful for permission to reproduce copyright material. Whilst every reasonable effort has been made to clear copyright and acknowledge sources, writers and artists, we would be happy to hear from any copyright holder not here acknowledged.

TEXT CREDITS

Margaret Drabble: from *The Millstone* published by Weidenfeld and Nicholson. © Margaret Drabble. Used by permission of Peters Fraser and Dunlop. Sally Emerson: from *Back to Work* from *Occasional Poets* published by Viking Penguin 1986. © 1983 Sally Emerson. Used by permission of Curtis Brown Ltd. Michele Guinness: from *Tapestry of Voices* published by SPCK, 1993. © 1993 Michele Guinness. Laurie Lee: from *Two Women* by Laurie Lee, © 1983 Laurie Lee, and *I Can't Stay Long* published by Andre Deutsch 1975. Reprinted by permission of Peters Fraser and Dunlop. Sue Limb: from *Love Forty* published by Corgi Books 1988, a division of Transworld Publishers Ltd. Groucho Marx: From *Love, Groucho* published by Faber and Faber. © 1992 Miriam Marx Allen. Hugh O'Neill: from *A Man Called Daddy* © 1996 Hugh O'Neill. Reprinted by permission of Rutledge Hill Press, Nashville. Nigel Planer: from *A Good Enough Dad* © 1992 Nigel Planer, published by Arrow Books. Reprinted by permission of Peters Fraser and Dunlop on behalf of Nigel Planer. Susanna Tamaro: from *Follow Your Heart* © 1994 Baldini & Castoldi, published by Random House Ltd. Reprinted with permission.

LIST OF ILLUSTRATIONS

Cover: *Baby sleeping on its back,* © 2000 Mel Yates, Pix S.A.

Title-page: *Adult and baby hands,* photographer unknown, Images Colour Library

Page 7: *Babies' feet,* photographer unknown, Images Colour Library

Page 9: *Portrait of a newborn in arms,* © 2000 Paul Venning, Pix S.A.

Page 11: *Mother kissing baby,* © 2000 Michael Goldman, Telegraph Colour Library

Page 13: *Adult's hand holding infant's hand,* © 2000 Terry Vine, Tony Stone Images

Page 15: Photographer unknown, Pictor International

Pages 16/17: *Father embracing baby (0-3 months),* © 2000 Joe Polollio, Tony Stone Images

Page 18: *Close-up of mother and baby (3 weeks),* © 2000 Dennis O'Clair, Tony Stone Images

Page 20: *Newborn baby up to mother in delivery room,* © 2000 Owen Franken, Tony Stone Images

Page 23: © 2000 John Olson, The Stock Market

Page 24: *Baby sleeping,* photographer unknown, Pix S.A.

Pages 26/27: *Four naked babies,* © 2000 Camille Tokerud, Tony Stone Images

Page 28: *Portrait of baby wearing white T-shirt,* © 2000 M. Hart, Pix S.A.

Pages 30/31: Photographer unknown, SuperStock

Page 32: *Back view of baby with hair sticking up on its head,* © 2000 Greg Bartley, Pix S.A.

Page 35: *Baby,* photographer unknown, Images Colour Library

Pages 36/37: *New-born baby,* © 2000 Genna Naccache, Pix S.A.

Page 38: *Naked baby leaning on his hands,* © 2000 Ed Horn, Pix S.A.

Page 41: *Baby swimming under water,* photographer unknown, Pictor International

Page 43: *Portrait of family, black father holding baby (3-6 months),* © 2000 Peter Correz, Tony Stone Images

Page 45: *Baby,* photographer unknown, Images Colour Library

Pages 46/47: *Portrait of three babies,* © 2000 Michele Salmieri, Pix S.A.

Pages 48/49: Photographer unknown, Pictor International

Page 51: Photographer unknown, Pictor International

Pages 52/53: Photographer unknown, SuperStock

Page 54: Photographer unknown, SuperStock

Page 57: *Child holding father's hand,* © Turner & Devries, The Image Bank

Page 58: *Chinese baby boy (6-9 months) crawling on floor,* © 2000 Camille Tokerud, Tony Stone Images

Page 60: *Baby asleep in mother's arms,* © 2000 Phil Borges, Tony Stone Images

Page 62: Photographer unknown, Pictor International

Page 64: © 2000 Jim Erickson, The Stock Market

Page 66: © 2000 Tom & DeeAnn McCarthy, The Stock Market

Page 68: Photographer unknown, Pictor International

Page 70: *Father holding baby (0-3 months) up to face,* © 2000 Donna Day, Tony Stone Images

Page 73: *Young mother and baby,* © 2000 Camille Tokerud, Tony Stone Images

Page 74: *Father with baby under water,* photographer unknown, Pictor International

Pages 76/77: *Crawling on wooden floor,* © 2000 Laurence Monneret, Tony Stone Images

Page 78: *White baby and black baby, sitting,* Pix S.A.

Page 81: *Baby,* photographer unknown, Images Colour Library

Page 82: © 2000 Nancy Ney, The Stock Market

Page 84: Photographer unknown, Pictor International

Pages 86/87: *Baby aged 15 months walking towards outstretched arms,* © 2000 Andy Cox, Tony Stone Images

Page 89: Photographer unknown, Pictor International

Page 90: *Two babies sitting,* © 2000 J. Albert, Pix S.A.

Page 93: *Close-up of baby,* © 2000 M. Malyszko, Pix S.A.

Page 95: *Baby wrapped in a towel,* photographer unknown, Images Colour Library

Page 97: Photographer unknown, Pictor International

Page 99: *Baby boy (0-3 months) sleeping,* © 2000 Dianne Flumara, Tony Stone Images

Page 101: © 2000 Brownie Harris, The Stock Market

Page 102: Photographer unknown, Images Colour Library

ABOUT THE AUTHOR

Helen Exley is one of the world's most successful anthologists. Her giftbooks of quotations on family relationships have sold over twenty-five million copies in thirty-seven languages, and she never tires of the joy of creating books.

Helen says of her new book *The Baby Blessing*, "The arrival of the new baby is an earth-shattering event for all concerned. A tiny baby is so vulnerable. So innocent. The event is so powerful in raw emotion that life will never be the same again. There is an absolute power in the helplessness of the new-born that bonds us for life."

Helen Exley has done a number of little books of quotations about babies (*Welcome to the New Baby*, for example), but she wanted to do a bigger book, something that would reflect the huge renewal in human life that comes through children. She and her researchers have been collecting the quotations for the book for seventeen years. Some of the quotations are by famous people, but many are from ordinary people who have written in to her over the years, telling of the overwhelming experiences of childbirth and raising children.

Helen believes that "the greatest contribution came in from my colleague Pam Brown, who in my view is the best writer of all on the subject of babies." When Helen felt the project was nearly ready, her team scoured the world for the most outstanding photographs, so that the book would be as universal as possible.

"This really is one of the most important subjects in the world," says Helen Exley. "If we could greet every child born with the love they deserve, so many of the problems of society would be resolved. When you see the devastating innocence of the young, it puts an entirely new edge on the reasons why we have to build a better world."

Helen Exley lives in Watford, England, and is C.E.O. of her own worldwide publishing company, which she runs with her husband, Richard.